TABLE OF CONTENTS

INTRODUCTION 1

CHAPTER 1: RAY KROC: HIS EARLY LIFE 3
The Early Life of a Salesman 3
Paper Cups and Mixers 10

CHAPTER 2: THE BROTHERS MCDONALD 17
The Hotdog Stand and the Pact of Being Millionaires by Fifty 17
Ray Kroc and the Dream That Became a Reality 23
Ray Kroc and McDonald's: The Ball Starts Rolling 29
1961: The Big Year 34

CHAPTER 3: RAY KROC: FAST FOOD KING 40
McDonald's Corporation: Ray Kroc a Man on a Mission 40

CHAPTER 4: THE RAY KROC LEGACY 49
Childhood Passion: From Hamburgers to Home Runs 49
Writing, Philanthropy, and Watching McDonald's Grow 51
The World That Cherished the King of Fast Food 53

CONCLUSION 56

INTRODUCTION

Ray Kroc.

That name, belonging to one of the most important men in the last 70 years, has become synonymous with a franchise whose brand is undoubtedly one of the most recognized across the world: McDonald's.

What he accomplished with the Big M has been so astonishing that one could say he alone revolutionized the way restaurants, or at least fast-food chains, operate. Quick, efficient, neat, professional, and sanitary, McDonald's has become an institution in its own right.

From the moment Ray Kroc first noticed the small restaurant in San Bernardino in 1954 which had been ordering his milkshake mixers - as he would see it - it was destiny or fate. It was something that felt so right. It was that moment of stunned silence where one thinks, "This deserves more. I want to give it more, make it more. I want to become a part of this. I can make this work." It was a moment of sudden clarity, of vision, of something that you see only once in your life: the chance to hold something so firmly in your grasp that you know it will not fail. Ray Kroc saw that in Richard and Maurice McDonald's restaurant.

And he did not fail.

What Ray Kroc accomplished with McDonald's is historical. He systematically revolutionized the way people looked at fast-food restaurants. He created an atmosphere at every single store that he opened - a sense of family. That he was able to ensure this vision of his became reality is extraordinary, a show of determination and never giving up. When Ray first met the McDonald brothers in 1954, he was already fifty-two. By the time he bought the brothers out of their own business, Ray was fifty-nine.

Ray was a colorful man, but there is no doubting that he was pure genius. His story is one of achieving great things despite one's age or background.

Ray Kroc was a man who said, "At home it's God, family, McDonald's. But at the office, it's McDonald's, family, God". The metamorphosis from salesman to fast-food franchise owner and real estate king is astounding. Throughout his life, Kroc was searching for opportunities - great ones - and that was something that he valued. He valued people's ideas and where they came from. Yes, the story of how he ended up with entire and absolute control over McDonald's as a whole is heartbreaking as he ruined the dreams of two brothers. But while he did do that, it was something he felt he simply had to do if he wanted to continue giving America McDonald's.

His story is incredible. His story is McDonald's.

Chapter 1

RAY KROC: HIS EARLY LIFE

The Early Life of a Salesman

On Sunday, October 5th, 1902, in a small town called Oak Park, near Chicago, Illinois, the man and business tycoon named Raymond Albert Kroc was born. He would be the oldest child of three, and the first son of two to be brought into the world by Alois "Louis" Kroc and Rose Mary Kroc (née Hrach).

Both Louis and Rose Mary were of Czech descent, with Louis from a village named Bøasy, Plzen, and Rose Mary an Illinois native, her mother and father originating from Czechoslovakia. Louis was a proponent of discipline, a man who prioritized, as was commonplace in those days, a cultivated culture of good manners, good behavior, and a presence that commanded respect. He worked for Western Union, the US telegraph company, where he would rise through the organization until he reached a well-paid position within the company. However, he would lose his entire fortune, which he acquired through speculating land in the 1920s, in the stock market crash of 1929, also known as the Great Depression, which strangled America into a state of anguish and plowed the nation into the ground. It should be said, though, that Louis Kroc was a baseball man, as big as they get. He had such a deep passion and love for the sport that it was inevitable that young Ray would soon follow in his footsteps.

Rose Mary, on the other hand, was an absolute treasure. She was a sweet and affectionate mother and she doted on Ray, who in turn paid that back tenfold. Rose was a homemaker by trade who supplemented her income by becoming a piano teacher, giving lessons to both children in the neighborhood and, it is safe to say, their parents and any other adults who were looking to learn to play the piano. Just as Ray's inherited burning passion for baseball was passed down to him by Louis, Ray was taught the piano, as one can expect, by Rose. Such was his intuitiveness for new opportunities and new interests, he learned the piano without too much difficulty. He had a fine voice to go with it, and Rose had said that Ray had a natural-born talent for the piano which she stated was something that made her proud and happy.

Interestingly, when Ray was just four years old, Louis took him to see a phrenologist, who determined that Ray would work in the food industry when he was older.

Ray had two other siblings. Robert, the middle child, and Lorraine, the youngest. Robert was born in 1907, while Lorraine was born in 1911, which put a considerable age difference between the three. Ray and Robert, when both of them were still young, felt the difference between them. Their interests differed immensely and they, as most young brothers do, failed to see eye-to-eye. Because of their differences they found it awkward and difficult to talk to each other. Robert was the academic type who performed well in school and had good grades. This certainly did not mean that Ray wasn't good at school, he simply did not apply himself. Ray did not see the importance of a fancy education - he, even then, was influenced by how he saw his father as an immigrant who made it in America. He saw his father's determination as the only way to succeed in life, the only way to achieve success. This sums up Ray Kroc - a determination to prove the doubters wrong, a persistence that said "it's not good enough", and a confidence that would shape him into the man he would become.

During his childhood, Ray was always scheming and came up with outlandish plots and plans in which to make those respective schemes work. He was somewhere between a schemer and a dreamer. After all, his nickname wasn't Danny Daydreamer for no reason. He was ambitious and showed a fundamental belief and core value that would stay with him for life:work hard, work until you can't, and work some more after that. But he had to start somewhere.

Ray stood out even at a young age. He was such a determined young boy that he became known for it throughout his neighborhood in Oak Park. He was very persistent, very persuasive, and he endeared himself in the feelings of others. They loved Ray, even though at times he could be a bit much. Such were the differences between him and Robert. Of course, they eventually found a median in adulthood, but Ray had a personality that relied on matching ambition. Robert was the academic one out of the three, but Ray never harbored any ill-feeling towards Robert for this. Ray was Ray and Robert was Robert. Ray respected the differences and admired his younger brother. Ray and Lorraine were very close, as any big brother would be with his younger sister. He was protective of her.

If there was one other thing in Ray's life that would come to define him as much as McDonald's would, it was baseball. Baseball was Louis's passion and that which he passed down to his son. Louis was a big fan of the Chicago Cubs and so Ray became a big fan of the Chicago Cubs.

Oak Park's Lincoln School, a grammar school, was Ray Kroc's first taste of being a salesman. He was a part of the debate team at Lincoln School and was quite brilliant at it, and he soon realized he had a natural talent for convincing folk easily, which, of course, is the salesman's most important tool. He knew how to sell himself, as well as his ideas and opinions. He showed incredible displays of quick thinking, which demonstrated his intelligence. He was called, on numerous occasions, "a very bright boy".

While at Lincoln, Ray started earning some money by doing odd jobs at drugstores and grocery stores in Oak Park. Sweeping, mopping, packing, and unpacking. Although he was content doing these odd jobs at the time, he wasn't altogether satisfied with the situation he was in. What he wanted to do was put his schemes and ideas into action, he wanted to realize the big dreams that he could so vividly visualize. So, he took his first step into the food business, selling lemonade outside of his home. He had a small stand and stood by that stand, where one can imagine the young boy convincing everyone that his lemonade was, by God, much better than the competition's.

But in 1916, as he entered his teenage years, Ray's thoughts were far from the days where he would do odd jobs and sell lemonade. In 1916, the whole of Europe had been stricken by the fear of the ongoing Great War and the repercussions this could have on the Continent. The United States of America, thus far avoiding the pleading glances of Britain and her allies to come to their aid in their time of need, was slowly succumbing to the realization that the nation's men would soon be shipping off to war-torn Europe. At this time, however, Ray Kroc was just fourteen, and his next big idea was becoming a reality. With two of friends, Ray opened up a music store named "Ray Kroc Music Emporium". His friends would sell the sheet music while Ray sat in a corner playing the piano. It started off well enough, but interest waned as Ray and his friends realized how hard it was to sustain a business and keep a store's doors open for business. Without the necessary experience and guidance, he failed to learn the sales side of the business, which demonstrated his youthful inexperience and innocence.

After a few short months, Ray Kroc's Music Emporium closed down. With Ray openly disappointed, he took up a job at his uncle's soda fountain. This was Ray Kroc's awakening to conducting sales with a smile and convincing people to buy much more than they had actually intended to. The lemonade stand had started to pay off. It his first real foray into the product industry he would soon find himself dedicating his sales talent to.

Soda fountains, a tap-based invention for the purpose of dispensing beverages (which are most commonly found being used in bars and cinemas today) have a largely colorful history. In the 1850s during the drug revolution, many people could be found in drugstores. People would visit drugstores for a drink to cure whatever it was that was affecting them. In those times, there were no laws put in place to govern the use of different medications and drugs that were often found in beverages. Caffeine, and even cocaine, were common ingredients in these beverages, with herbs and different flavoring agents used as well. But, with this, the first soda fountain could be found in the 1880s. A man named Jacob Baur came up with the idea that soda fountains nowadays have become so synonymous with - carbon dioxide-filled tanks. This allowed for many shops to incorporate carbonated soft drinks into their inventory.

By the time World War I broke out in 1914, the United States' national congress passed a law which stated that over-the-counter drugs, such as cocaine and opiates, were officially banned. The new law was passed because people were becoming increasingly disconcerted with the prospect of consuming addictive and intoxicating drugs in their beverages. This made it difficult for Baur to promote his new invention - the "healthier" and friendlier carbonated beverages. However, Baur succeeded, and by the time Ray was working at his uncle's soda fountain in 1916, the soda fountain industry was starting to pick up.

It was at this drugstore soda fountain that Ray Kroc began learning the importance of having people skills and playing to the crowd's ears. He learned that even though what he was selling was only carbonated drinks, it was an opportunity.

But a year later, that opportunity changed into an entirely different one. On April 6th, 1917, the United States joined Britain, France, and Russia. This came after Germany announced it would resume its campaign of unrestricted warfare in war-zone waters. Three days after the announcement, the United States severed all diplomatic ties with Germany, with an announcement from the US government that they would be joining the war fluttering around shortly afterward.

For Ray Kroc, who by now was just fifteen and just out of his sophomore year, his new opportunity was to fight for his country. However, due to his age, he could not join the army, so, after lying about his age, he joined the American Red Cross where he served as an ambulance driver. He dropped out of school to serve his country, but Ray (as we know) wasn't too concerned about his schooling to begin with. Ray desperately wanted to serve on the front line in France and, after he was sent to Connecticut for his training, that ambition was seemingly closer than ever.

Interestingly, while still undergoing his training in Connecticut, Ray met with another young boy who had, like Ray, also faked his age to join the cause for his country. This young man was viewed as a bit strange, different. He was very artistic and failed to take an interest in the inhibitions that the other young men around him had, such as drinking and chasing girls during furlough. Ray noticed how the young man would prefer to be by himself, sketching and visually realizing his ideas onto a sheet of paper. Ray eventually become friendly with the young man and soon learned that his name was Walter Elias. Walter Elias, you see, would become even more iconic than his new friend Raymond Kroc. Walter Elias, with all his sketching and drawing, would persevere through tough times to become more famously known as Walt Disney. Even more, when Ray began franchising McDonald's for Richard and Maurice McDonald, Ray sent a letter to Walt Disney asking if Walt would be interested in opening a McDonald's at his new amusement park, Disneyland. Ray did not receive a reply back.

(Along with this comes another topic for discussion. Ray was not the only Oak Park resident riding in an ambulance. There was an ambulance driver by the name of Ernest Hemingway, the famous author and journalist.)

But, as fate would have it, just before he was to ship out overseas, the First World War ended. Soon, he was back home to Chicago, Illinois.

Shortly after returning home from Connecticut, Louis sat Ray down and insisted that Ray finish his schooling at Lincoln School. Louis was adamant that Ray have something in the form of education to show for himself, which Louis persisted was invaluable for his son. Ray was apprehensive at first, but he relented and abided by his father's wish. So Ray Kroc returned to school. The dreamer within him was still burning strong and his own personal ambitions - and possibly outlook on life - resumed. He lasted just one semester before he dropped out of school for good. Ray had other plans which he knew would come to fruition, so he let that old feeling take hold:that an education did not apply to real-life nor to real-world American success. Ray Kroc had the skills that he believed would propel him into a successful and accomplished life. He knew what he wanted to do and how to make his plan - his vision for himself - work. But things were not going to be as easy as he thought.

Ray began his career as a salesman in 1919 when he was 17 years old. He also had other side jobs which contributed to his income, as he landed a gig as a pianist at a club, and he worked as a DJ for a radio station in Oak Park. His life at that time was very centered around music, his mother's musical influence showing its passion through Ray. It was also around this time that he met Ethel Fleming. They quickly fell in love and started dating. He never really settled in on a job in those early years. Ray simply wanted more. He wanted more excitement, more "bigger" opportunities to show up. He had the drive, the ambition. He had the dreams, the will, the charm, and the correct characteristics to get to the top. But the top of what? One thing he knew from those days on the debate team at Lincoln School - he would make a swell salesman. He also loved the idea of family. His father had told Ray that in order to get married he needed to find a job. With Ray's outgoing and natural salesman's charm he landed a job with the Lily Tulip Paper Cup Company.

Paper Cups and Mixers

Ray Kroc dipped his hands into an assorted array of sales-related markets; everything from becoming a real estate agent in Fort Lauderdale to selling products for women. When that wasn't enough he landed a job in New York with the American Stock Exchange where he worked as a ticker-tape reader and in the ASE's symbols translation. It was only in 1923, when he was twenty-one years old, that Ray found a steady job in sales that he felt was incredibly well-suited for him to prosper.

This sales job came in the form of selling paper cups for the Lily Tulip Paper Cup Company. For Ray, the job was right up his alley. He put into practice his confidence, determination, ambition, and charm, and this environment created within Ray a sense of belonging. A sense that he was doing what he knew how to do best - sell. He was able to travel around the United States (which by this time was suffering from the stock market crash), meet new people, and make some money. Ray Kroc was in his element.

In 1924, Ethel gave birth to Marilyn, a beautiful baby girl. Ray felt renewed and although he was just twenty-two, he also felt mature enough to make things work. His parents were supportive, and this made Ray a bit more comfortable with the situation. Now he was married to the woman that he loved and a father to a gorgeous little girl. He had a stable job. Ray was settled. But Ray, of course, could hardly formulate the word "settled"; it did not have a place in his vocabulary. The only downside to being on the road so much was the fact that he had to leave behind his wife and his few months old baby daughter. Not one for emotion - stoic at best - Ray stayed focused on the job at hand. He wanted to provide for his young family, and that's exactly what Ray did.

There was another side to Ray which made him look humble in the eyes of his customers. Fatherhood had seemingly enhanced his "scheming, nice guy" persona, bringing out a touch of "I'm gonna look after you" in his sales style. He was dedicated not only to the job but to the people - his customers - who helped Ray make a living and put a roof over Ethel and their daughter's heads. He was always on-hand to cater to his customers at the drop of a hat. It is no surprise, then, that after a very short while, Ray was viewed as one of the best salesmen at the Lily Tulip Paper Cup Company, eventually rising to become the Midwest's sales manager.

Ray was a very capable young man and he desperately wanted to succeed at everything that he did. He put his mind to everything that he did and developed the habit of believing in big ideas. As was the case when he was a child, he dreamed up schemes and businesses and visualized himself being the successful man he aspired to be. This made him quite critical of himself and he put his heart into everything that he did. Whether at home with Ethel and Marilyn, or at work making and closing sales, so as to avoid the feeling of detachment that he was prone to. He always saw the big picture, even if it meant he had to risk everything, and so he developed a sense of never being afraid. This would serve him well throughout his life. He was not one for conflict but he would not sit back and take punches.

He was a very dedicated young man, partly due to the family life he was exposed to when he was younger. The Kroc family were seen as the model American family. This overlapped into his adulthood. Everything he did was for Ethel and Marilyn.

But in 1938, the now thirty-six-year-old Ray became unsettled after fifteen years with the paper cup company due to that feeling of wanting a bigger opportunity. He met a man named Earl Prince, a small ice cream shop owner and one of Ray's contacts. Ray listened to the man's story. There was something, though, that had Ray hooked in an instant. Earl Prince spoke about his new invention and Ray knew then and there that he wanted to be a part of it, seeing the bright lights of opportunity take center stage. The invention, as Earl Prince explained, was something he had named the "Multimixer". Essentially, the Multimixer was a milkshake mixer. However, and unlike most conventional milkshake makers that only had one spindle, the Multimixer had five spindles. This intrigued Ray. Most milkshakes take a while to get to you, Prince continued, when one place or the other is having a busy day. The Multimixer would cut that waiting period five to one. It was all about efficiency, serving the customers by the handful in one go. It was all about decreasing the time in which it took to make something as simple as a milkshake and by decreasing the time, multiplying the number of milkshakes someone could make. Decrease the waiting time for each paying customer and increase the number of milkshakes rolling out.

Ray, in his usual way, saw the potential in Earl Prince's invention. He calculated and processed every single aspect of the product and the impact it could have on the food industry. He quickly came to the conclusion that Multimixers were the future of the food industry, allowing increased productivity in less time. He firmly believed that, in no time at all, restaurants and the like across the country would be pining to make use of this incredible invention.

Ray stuck it out for another year at Lily Tulip Paper Cup Company before he got that old itch again. Earl Prince's invention had stayed on his mind and created - once again - a feeling within Ray that this was "the one". Multimixers were the Promised Land of sales. It was going to be a gold mine, he told himself. Ethel, on the other hand, must have felt a bit disgruntled at her husband's unsettled behavior. By this time things were comfortable and settled - they had a house, they had money - not a lot, but they got by. Ray had returned to Lily Tulip Paper Cup Company to resume his job selling paper cups after a disastrous spell trying to sell land in Florida that had left him close to losing everything. So why the change? Why the risk?

But Ray, even though he was now approaching his forties, was his same old determined and ambitious self. After sixteen years of selling paper cups, Ray got in touch with Earl Prince, who gave Ray the exclusive marketing rights of the Multimixer. The salesman turned visionary businessman, Ray and Earl formed the Prince Castle Sales company. He deserted his stable job selling paper cups to venture into the universe of selling five-spindle milkshake mixers. This needed to be the one.

At first, the Multimixers were a hit. As Ray had predicted, people were queuing up for them. In a good year, Prince Castle Sales were selling somewhere in the region of 7500 to 8000 mixers a year. However, as the years rolled by, interest in the mixers waned and ebbed and dwindled on borderline humiliating.

Along with fierce competition from other mixer companies - and once World War II had come to its conclusion - America became a much more fast-paced country. When the war ended, a new culture rose up overnight and that culture was the youthful diversity of entitlement. Young men and women felt like they were the conquers of evil and were entitled to a more fast-paced environment in which to grow. They wanted the country to move with them, to pick up speed, and move forward in new directions.

The Multimixer was a hit upon its release in the US market. By the end of the Second World War, a new bill was passed by the US government - the G.I Bill - which allowed for houses to be purchased by individuals at a lower interest rate. Coupled with this was the sudden boom in the automobile industry and the construction of the Interstate Highway, which allowed people to go into suburban areas from the highway. Now people wanted to be a part of the suburban revolution. Ray noticed how the quick shift from cities to the suburbs had taken place. This had an effect on how well the Multimixer business was going, with it suddenly dipping low due to the effect of this suburban shift on the food industry in the cities. However, Ray was a calculated man, and even though the food industry was taking a hit, Ray utilized his experience to keep the wheels turning.

Things began to change rapidly as more and more new trends began to pop up across the country. Restaurants and soda fountains - which were Ray's main customer based - took a hit, with mixer sales dropping exponentially. More worryingly, was how these restaurants and soda fountains were feeling the effects of drive-ins, a convenient system that met the faster moving, youth-driven nation's approval by serving people their meals straight to their cars. But these drive-ins, though hugely popular, became a breeding ground for what one could term "undesirable" behavior. Teenagers, mostly car-crazed tuners, would frequent these places and smoke and drink, often creating an unfriendly atmosphere for families. Family was important to Ray, and he felt despairingly toward this new culture. But, again, everything for Ray Kroc was an opportunity to see things differently, to find the opportunity at the bottom of the muddied pit.

The years came and went. Business was still taking a hit. Sales continued to dip. The mixers were losing their appeal, and Ray was only just getting by with what he was earning, which stemmed from selling - if he was lucky - three to four mixers a month, a considerable monthly percentage drop in comparison to the golden days of selling almost eight thousand mixers a year.

So, in 1954, when Ray was told that a small restaurant in San Bernardino, California wanted several of his Multimixers, he initially did not believe it. He phoned the restaurant in San Bernardino to clear things up and let them know that there was a mistake on their order. A man named Richard McDonald answered the phone, who in fact, told Ray that, yes, the order was right, that the number of mixers ordered was correct. This stunned Ray but also brought him back up from the many lows he had been going through and suffering from emotionally and financially. He just couldn't believe that a restaurant was so busy that they would need to be making thirty-five to forty milkshakes at a time. No way in hell was that possible. Or even close to reality. So Ray plotted his course and headed to San Bernardino. He had to see it for himself. He had to see what kind of establishment needed so many mixers.

He had always seen and been a big believer in taking opportunities with both hands, but nothing could have prepared Ray for what would unfold.

Little did he know that in San Bernardino, his life would change forever. At fifty-two years old, Ray Kroc would be taking his first steps towards a revolution which he would set in motion. At fifty-two years old, Ray Kroc's life was only just getting started, the big opportunity he had for so long craved presented itself in the most unlikely of places. From Chicago to California, his journey was just beginning.

Chapter 2

THE BROTHERS MCDONALD

The Hotdog Stand and the Pact of Being Millionaires by Fifty

The true story about the franchise we know today as McDonald's can be traced back to 1937. Two brothers, Richard and Maurice McDonald, more affectionately known as Dick and Mac, moved from New Hampshire to Hollywood, California, where they worked as stagehands in studios. Dick and Mac ended up opening their own movie theatre in Monrovia. But something wasn't right - business was slow and they were hardly turning a profit. As fate would have it, they opened up a hotdog stand in Monrovia, California. Dick and Mac were fixated by the success of a vendor who had also been selling hotdogs from a stand just across the street. This hotdog stand seemed to be the only business that was making a profit at all in the area, so Dick and Mac decided to do the same, seeing the potential in selling hotdogs. However, the brothers McDonald's hotdog stand didn't pick up quite as much as they had initially hoped. They realized that they had built their business in such a way that it catered to the needs of folks who were down at the racetrack, and once the racing season ended, the customers were rare. The pact that they had made to each other, that they would both be millionaires by the time that they were 50, seemed a long, long way away, and an unrealistic dream. But they didn't give up.

This could be when Maurice slowly started seeing the flaws in their business, or rather where their business was based. Monrovia was a small town with a small population and most businesses in the Monrovia area struggled to turn a profit. Maurice mentioned his new idea to Richard, who mulled it over and agreed with his brother. The decision made, Richard and Maurice moved eastwards to San Bernardino, which had a far larger population than Monrovia with approximately 100,000 inhabitants. San Bernardino was a working-class town with good folk, and this appealed to both Dick and Mac.

But this new adventure to the east did not go so smoothly. First, they needed a loan in order to raise the basic funds for restarting their hotdog stand. A handful of banks declined Dick and Mac's applications to get a loan. They felt as if they were down and out until the Bank of America approved the loan. So in 1940, three years after opening their first hotdog stand, and with $5,000 in capital to reopen their venture, Dick and Mac McDonald finally opened up their new drive-in restaurant. After a few months, it started picking up and continued to grow until the $5,000 loan from the Bank of America had paid off exponentially. Dick and Mac's restaurant was making on average $40,000 a year, which was some big money. Their business had become a success, and even Dick and Mac were both surprised and taken aback by such success. One can imagine their humility, that steady determination to just continue and get on with it. They had a pact and a dream that needed realizing.

The crowds that the drive-in restaurant, which served everything from hotdogs and hamburgers to lemonade and milkshakes, was pulling in were mostly teenagers and young men in their 20s. The reason behind this was the one thing that often made such restaurants such a success: the carhops, young, beautiful women, who brought out and served the food. But what made Dick and Mac really think about changing their current business model was the one crowd that deeply appealed to them and what they wanted to do with the atmosphere of the restaurant: young families. Dick and Mac liked to see young families come in. They wanted to attract families and create a family-friendly establishment where families could enjoy a meal together. To accomplish this, they had to rethink and restructure McDonald's.

Dick and Mac had observed the way their business had been run for years, always looking at the kind of crowds it attracted, and after a few years decided that the restructuring process they had thought about needed to come into effect sooner rather than later. The first aspect of their business that they looked at was redesigning how they served their customers. The first question was, "Do we need carhops?" Their answer was no. The carhops, though good for business, were not so good at their jobs. They would take a long time to get and take orders in and out due to their tendency to flirt with the young customers. This was undesirable behavior and made the carhop model inefficient, unreliable, and hard to communicate and deal with. They decided to drop the carhops, which they hoped would drive the ill-behaved young men and their inhibitions away as well, which it did. What Dick and Mac also did not want was smoking or drinking on the premises. They hoped that their adjustments to the model would swiftly bring about change.

But then, after closer inspection, Dick and Mac saw that they had too many useless food choices on their menu. They looked at what had sold and what had not and Dick and Mac came to the conclusion that hamburgers were the most popular item; they made up a large percentage of their restaurant's total sales. They looked at the upkeep of the appliances which they used to make the hamburgers - they were easier to clean and worked a bit better. They also realized that making a hamburger was much less time consuming than the other items on their menu.

So, in 1948, eight years after opening the new drive-in in San Bernardino, the brothers renovated their restaurant, customer service, and menu. Their main focus now was on hamburgers, french fries, and milkshakes. Dick and Mac wanted something that would stand out from the rest, that would cost less to operate but bring in a bit more money, and that would keep their dream alive. What they did achieve was a new McDonald's Hamburger that became something quite different during that time in America, which was still transitioning after the war.

While the basis of McDonald's was like all other drive-ins and restaurants where the patrons arrive by car, McDonald's surprisingly, and quite confusingly to the patrons, did not have a dining area where they could eat. This wasn't a new way of doing things for Dick and Mac as they had also deliberately avoided having a dining area when they had the hotdog stand. What also stood out was that there was no waiting staff. This meant that the patrons had to come and order their food at the front window, which the food was also delivered through. The kitchen, however, was the brothers' innovation at its finest. They famously rebuilt their kitchen for the purpose of more efficiency, where the staff could make the burgers, fries, and milkshakes as if the meals were being mass-produced off of an assembly line. The layout was flawless, and it was much more efficient.

The burgers themselves were pre-cooked ahead of time to be prepared for the peak rush times and then kept warm so as not to miss a beat when things got busy. The french fries were even kept warm with the technique of using infrared lighting. This was efficiency of the highest level which made preparation of the food quick and easy, cutting the time of making a full meal from thirty minutes like most restaurants to thirty seconds. This was the beginning of the "Speedie System™", which has today become the hallmark of fast-food restaurants. The system the brothers had invented was historic and would become iconic today. In a faster moving country that was full of determination and grit post-war, the McDonald's brothers created a restaurant that was up to the exact specifications of fast-paced America, making them family-oriented *and* convenient.

Dick and Mac's pact to make a million dollars before they turned fifty was on, now with the success of McDonald's prevailing and continuing right before their eyes. Their idealism of a family friendly restaurant was in place, and the growth of the restaurant itself allowed for Dick and Mac to start thinking bigger. One of those bigger ideas was the Speedie System™ itself. They decided to make the Speedie System™ an entity, so they began franchising the system in 1953. The starting point for the system was in Phoenix, Arizona, at a restaurant owned by a gentleman named Neil Fox. It worked very well at Mr. Fox's operation, so Dick and Mac discussed something else that had become a new feature on the agenda - franchising the whole McDonald's name rather than just the Speedie System™. For this, they teamed up with an architect named Stanley Clark Meston, who helped design the new restaurants with the same standard core as the original McDonald's in San Bernardino. This new restaurant, however, would have something never seen before at any restaurant of any size and shape in America and possibly the world - two golden arches on either side of the building, which, if viewed from a certain angle, would appear to be a golden "M".

Things got very complicated for Dick and Mac when they realized that at the other restaurants the operators had added things to the standard and well-polished menu. They also discovered that these restaurants were filthy, with litter strewn about, and "undesirable" crowds frequenting. Cigarette buds lay on the floor, while beer bottles sat in young men's hands. No families were present. This infuriated Dick and Mac, who soon realized that the one factor that they had not thought about was the impossible task of control over these branches. With the distances between them, things were bound to get lost in translation and ignored. The McDonald's brothers sat and discussed this for a long time and ultimately gave up on the idea of expansion. They left the McDonald's branches alone so that they could focus on their restaurant in San Bernardino.

Back in San Bernardino, McDonald's was hugely popular and hugely successful. It was even featured in newspapers and magazines due to its success. Business was picking up and the brothers became content with how things were going. They did not want to get ahead of themselves and decided to be patient.

In 1954, a year after their plans of franchising had seemingly failed, they realized the huge demand for milkshakes that they were getting. Dick placed an order through Prince Castle Sales for several of their five-spindled milkshake mixers, the Multimixer. Soon, though, Dick received a phone call from one of the salesmen at Prince Castle, who thought that they had made a mistake with the order. Dick reassured the salesman, who addressed himself as Ray Kroc, that he had, in fact, placed the correct order.

What the brothers did not know was that the ambitious salesman on the other end of the line would be in San Bernardino a few days later to see for himself the restaurant that ordered so many Multimixers. What they also did not know was that Ray Kroc would change their business and their lives forever. The salesman would arrive with love in his eyes and an instant feeling of opportunity engulfing him. This would, though, engulf the McDonald brothers dream and tarnish that dream for good.

Ray Kroc and the Dream That Became a Reality

Ray Kroc, still bemused by the order of eight Multimixers from a little restaurant called McDonald's in San Bernardino, caught a flight out to California and took a drive to McDonald's. He was still unsure of the order that had been placed and found it unlikely that these people would need to be making forty milkshakes at one time. Five milkshakes at a time? That he could understand. But forty? Who did they think they were? Either they were America's most successful "unknown" backwater restaurant or these guys were just plain crazy.

He drove around until he saw it. And there it was, on the corner of 1398 North E Street and West 14th Street, that Ray Kroc got out of his car and stared long and hard at the sight before him. This tiny, unassuming, octagonal-shaped establishment with all-glass walls and all-male staff clad in white uniforms and white hats, was packed. The car lot was full of cars and queues of people lining up for some food. Ray Kroc told TIME Magazine in 1973: "When I got there, I saw more people waiting in line than I had ever seen at any drive-in. I said to myself: 'Son of a bitch, these guys have got something. How about if I open some of these places?'"

Eight Multimixers seemed about right.

What Ray was so stunned by was how simple the place was. The joint was such an innovative operation that he ended up falling in love right then and there. Ray Kroc had just laid his eyes on the one opportunity that would make him a billionaire. But he was surprised that for a place that only served hamburgers, french fries, and milkshakes, it was incredibly popular. As he mentioned it was the biggest line of people he had ever seen at a drive-in.

For Ray, he saw the potential in the McDonald's restaurant. He spoke with both brothers about their story and how this incredible restaurant came to be what it was. Ray stressed the importance of the family-style way the restaurant was being operated, with, as he noted, no young guns roaming around smoking and drinking and flirting with carhops. He was astounded at how people adapted to this new way of getting meals - by simply walking up to a window, placing your order, and getting it in such a short time, still hot, and delicious. He also pointed out how consistent the process was when it came to churning out the exact same meal - it never tasted different, it did not taste any better or worse than the last one. It was just… perfect. All of it. It was above and beyond all and every expectation. It maintained the standard that the McDonald brothers prioritized and were proud of.

For starters, McDonald's offered a menu with only nine items on it - burgers, french fries, shakes, and pies. They took the dining area out of the equation entirely and used paper and plastic wrapping, bags, and cups which you could simply throw away after use, instead of the usual glass and china that inhabited every other restaurant. Fifteen cent burgers and ten cent fries? Ray had visions of what the restaurant could be.

Ray Kroc, staring at that building, at the line of people - young and old, men and women, children of all ages - eagerly waiting for their McDonald's hamburger, fries, and shakes, saw his destiny rush towards him with one mouthful. He saw the establishment of McDonald's for what it was and what it could be. Furthermore, he saw himself being involved in the business. He saw himself using this fine restaurant as a way for him to sell more mixers. But he also saw so much more than just that.

Ray was not going to let this one slip through his fingers. During one of their conversations, Ray put forward an offer to Dick and Mac the very next day. Ray Kroc offered the McDonald brothers his expertise in sales, selling an idea, making people feel like they are a part of that idea. He offered to work as a franchising agent for McDonald's, with a cut of the profits that they made. The brothers were at first hesitant, but they decided it might be a good idea. They had learned from their prior experiences with selling rights in Phoenix and Sacramento, that they were best suited to run their operation in San Bernardino, and Kroc became a conduit through which to do that whilst franchising McDonald's as a whole entity. They were still hesitant about the salesman who claimed he had a vision and big plans for their restaurant. But this seemed like too great an opportunity for them to pass up.

They struck a deal which stated that Ray would sell McDonald's franchises for $950, an incredibly cheap price. Upon each sale, he would take 1.4% of the profit and give the brothers a third of that, with Dick and Mac receiving 0.5% of the profits. That meant they only earned 1.9% of total sales the franchises would make, which was barely sustainable. However, despite Ray's bigger percentage of the profits, this was hardly enough to get by with anything. Most of the proceeds he earned would go back into McDonald's - for marketing, costs, and his overheads, which included all the traveling. The McDonald brothers, in-tune with their current system, were only supplementing their income. By this time, McDonald's was earning $100,000 yearly, and the brothers were quite comfortable with the situation.

Ray became incredibly desperate for this venture to succeed. With his age not going in reverse, he felt he was too old to restart his career. He had left Prince Castle to be a partner with the McDonald brothers, but he harbored deep-seated anxiety underneath his hard, salesman exterior. Ray was worried about losing everything he had worked so hard for over the last thirty years. His house in Arlington Heights back home in Illinois and his life with Ethel, who was growing more and more disgruntled with Ray each day.

Meanwhile, the brothers would focus more on their restaurant while Ray handled the franchising and business side of McDonald's. Ray always had big dreams and in this case they aligned with Dick and Mac's dreams. Although their "millionaires by fifty" pact had not worked out so well, with Dick now fifty-two years old (the same age as Ray was in 1954, as both men were born in 1902 just one month apart), they were still just as determined to make it as ever.

Ray had the experience, knowledge, and know-how when it came to the food industry. While he was selling the paper cups for Lily Tulip Paper Cup Company and the mixers for Prince Castle, he saw a lot of restaurants, diners, ice cream shops, and coffee shops. As he said in an interview, "I considered myself a connoisseur of kitchens. I prided myself on being able to tell which operations would appeal to the public and which would fail."

But things in Ray's personal life were starting to break down. Ethel, his wife since 1922, was becoming unhappy with the amount of time her husband spent away from home, as Ray was constantly bustling around the country, chasing his many dreams which had never worked out. She was beginning to feel a sense of neglect, that she was the one who was settled and that Ray was the one who was unsettled. She had a volatile personality, as did Ray, and he told her that McDonald's was the future. He knew he had to be a part of it. And now that he was, as their franchising agent, he was not going to allow himself to stop until he was satisfied with the work that he had done for Dick and Mac. He understood the risks of getting the business side of McDonald's to the top, but he had a vision, and that vision, God willing, would not fail. He knew it couldn't, he had already seen how popular the joint was in San Bernardino. This was the highest kind of motivation, and he would need a hell of a lot if he was going to pull this off. He had Dick and Mac's approval and confidence, which motivated him further.

All that was left to be done was to begin his work.

What he wanted to do with McDonald's was big. Coast to coast, the biggest restaurant chain in history. Essentially, what Ray wanted to do was grow the restaurant into a chain, cultivate thousands of McDonald's around America, and expand to the point where there were many McDonald's restaurants in each and every state in the United States of America. But Ray was frustratingly brought back down to earth when Dick and Mac said that they only wished to maintain a small number of restaurants.

There is something about Ray Kroc that makes people think about how much he did to get to where he ended up, and it is quite astonishing just how much he actually did. McDonald's as we know it today would not be the McDonald's we're familiar with if we took the Ray Kroc factor out of the equation. Without Ray Kroc, there would be no McDonald's as we know it. To put it simply, McDonald's is Ray Kroc. He slowly built a fast-food giant that would change the world in terms of the impact it had on the food industry.

Ray saw things like no one else could. He is what we could describe as a "doer". He was motivated and boy, did he get things done. The first time he saw McDonald's in 1954 in San Bernardino and instantly fell in love. He saw the future of the small, well-operated, well-polished restaurant and in a few years had accomplished the future he dreamed of. Of course, it is difficult to truly understand what exactly went through his mind that day in San Bernardino, but from what he accomplished, we can slowly begin to piece together the Ray Kroc puzzle. He was ambitious enough to approach Dick and Mac McDonald with his proposal to help them franchise McDonald's, to get McDonald's "coast to coast". Even after they explained to him that they had already tried and failed to franchise, this seemingly motivated Ray even more to succeed. He was not deterred by their revelation of failure. Why? Because he knew that he was the right man for the job. He simply knew that he could get it done. This was bigger than selling paper cups, and this was bigger than selling Multimixers. This was the biggest opportunity that he had ever seen, and he knew that he was going to get the job acting as their franchising agent and succeed in this role. Which, of course, he did. Undoubtedly, he succeeded with flying colors.

By this time, Ray was feeling quite lonely. He was on the road all the time, traveling across the United States to either scout new locations or to have meetings with franchisees. He was busy and it kept him from home. He did feel guilty about this, but he also knew that this was his calling. McDonald's was becoming his life. That was not his fault, as he saw it. It wasn't anyone's fault. It was just one of those things. But he knew things would be difficult. He felt that was just the price to pay in order for someone to become successful in whatever it is that they do. Nobody ever said that one could follow an easy road to become successful. Ray lived by this mantra. And because of this mantra, he traveled the difficult road which would allow him to find his long-awaited success. He persevered. He persisted. He understood. His experience and knowledge were put into practice so as to make sure everything went according to the plan that he laid down for himself, and that plan was to establish the foundations for McDonald's to flourish across America. In this, he could not fail. He could not afford to.

But he continued on his journey and, though by now feeling the effects of his miserly 1.4%, he still made things happen. He consistently found ways in which to make things work, and that alone is what makes him stand out. He was so focused on and dedicated to the task at hand that he did not for one second allow himself to be put down by his own emotions or the hesitancy of others. Ray Kroc put his own issues in life aside so that he could invest one hundred percent of himself into making McDonald's what it deserved to be.

As it always was with Ray, ever since childhood, he saw the big picture. And for him, McDonald's was not only the big picture but also the future -

his future - and he planned to spread that future across the country. Whether or not he succeeded relied on how well he could sell the idea of McDonald's to others. Again, he had to explain to potential investors and franchisees why McDonald's would stand out amongst the competitors popping up on the playing field of the fast-food business. He had to use every ounce of experience as a salesman so as to persuade them to buy into McDonald's as he did. What he saw in McDonald's - that potential to become something truly special that everyone in America could enjoy - he wanted everyone else to see that as well, and he knew that he had to work even harder in order to achieve that.

Of course, Ray knew he was fifty-two years old and that most men his age were already thinking about retirement. But not him. For Ray, he was just getting started. He knew that this one was "the one". McDonald's was something special. While fifty-two was supposed to be the time of his life where he went through the motions of his golden years, all he could think about were those golden arches. What Ray wanted to do was make food fast. Faster than it had ever been.

Ray Kroc and McDonald's: The Ball Starts Rolling

With the deal done and Dick and Mac onboard with Ray's ideas, he began the process of franchising McDonald's in the hopes of it becoming just as special to America as it was to him. He knew what he had to do, and what he needed above everything was for his vision of a future McDonald's - the future of McDonald's - coupled with the risk that he had taken to work. He needed it to work out. His aim was to have McDonald's coast to coast in America.

The first piece of the puzzle would be to open his first McDonald's. The whole chain's livelihood relied on this one restaurant. The one Ray would open, after haggling with the banks to secure a loan for the building of the establishment, was located closer to home - Des Plaines, Illinois. This one would be viewed as an "experimental" model of the McDonald's format. It would feature the same prices, same menu, and same efficient service as its sister stand in San Bernardino. Opening day, much to Ray's relief, was a hit, with the restaurant racking up $366 in sales on its first day.

This store Ray would treat as if it were his church. He performed all the chores himself at night once it closed for the day. People remember seeing him sweeping outside, using a knife to scrape gum off that had been discarded on the parking lot. He treated the Des Plaines McDonald's with the utmost respect. He was trying to keep the idea that Dick and Mac had sold to him - that McDonald's is always presentable, sanitary, and friendly. Ray did a commendable job overseeing the transition of expansion to Illinois, with it his deep appreciation for Dick and Mac's model. Ray wanted to keep it as authentic as possible. Even when scouting locations for his stores later on during the massive boom of McDonald's popping up everywhere, Ray would have the company plane fly over suburban areas and look for church steeples. His thinking was that wherever there were churches there were good American families.

But, obviously, Des Plaines was just the start. It was the first link in Ray's vision to franchise McDonald's across America. And to do that he had to enforce the rule book during this time to - again - keep McDonald's as authentic as possible. He simply did not want the other stores he would open to lose that feeling, the family-oriented atmosphere, the cleanliness, or the nine-item menu. He needed to run a tight ship and he certainly knew this after learning about Dick and Mac's failure to preside over the other stores when they first attempted to franchise. Discipline was needed to get this message through. Discipline to keep McDonald's going smoothly and discipline to enhance the image of McDonald's. And this was no different than refining the procedure of constructing a hamburger.

That authenticity to conform to a single model, a single procedure, was the smartest move Ray made - keeping the patties exactly the way they were. And his hamburgers were to be made with nothing short of pin-point accuracy. Burger Patty weight should be 1.6 ounces exactly; diameter should be 3.875 inches exactly; fat content should be below 19 percent exactly; a teaspoon of mustard, exactly; a tablespoon of ketchup, exactly; a quarter ounce of onions... exactly. With this in mind, one should note that Ray Kroc devised "hamburgerology" in the late 1950s, the McDonald's "university" training for staff who were going to join the company. Ray Kroc embodied the McDonald's authenticity. After all, he did famously say, "There is a science to making and serving a hamburger."

In 1955, with things starting to go well for Ray, he set up the McDonald's Systems, Inc, which later became the McDonald's Corporation, so he would have control and billing over the franchising of McDonald's. However, this is where Ray started to become so obsessed with the company that he began to view himself as the founder of McDonald's, famously and controversially labeling the Des Plaines, Illinois McDonald's as "McDonald's #1". He completely failed to credit Dick and Mac McDonald or their San Bernardino restaurant. But things with Dick and Mac had become a constant strain for Ray due to their modesty and failure to see his vision of their own business. It frustrated Ray, and this can be viewed as the moment when Ray Kroc became Mr. McDonald's, the man who would build an empire, especially with the inclusion of Harry J. Sonneborn who came to his aid.

1955 was also a struggle for Ray. Other players in the fast-food business were still doing pretty well for themselves. InstaBurger (later Burger King) had opened its doors at the same time as Ray started selling his idea of

McDonald's to potential investors and franchisees (who, with authenticity to the McDonald's, were usually married couples to further set in stone the family atmosphere). Ray had to graft like never before with his sales pitches and speeches about why McDonald's was the business to be involved with. But, as Ray always did, he convinced people that they should be with McDonald's and showed them respect rather than an aura of "you work for me, son." He was so immensely likable despite that arrogance that could easily be mistaken for endearing charm.

By 1959, Ray had opened store number one hundred. Yet still, that 1.4% was taking its toll on Ray. The upkeep was immense and it was hurting him financially. His diabetes and arthritis were also becoming a pain, but he didn't let that stop him. He could have thrown the towel in at any point but Ray was so devoted to McDonald's and the vision he had for it, that he worked even harder. Now fifty-seven, Ray Kroc was just getting warmed up. But even then, in 1959, he was running out of ideas. That all changed when he met Harry Sonneborn, former vice president of finance at Tastee-Freez, who put forward to Ray a proposition (or in Ray's case, a solution) which would benefit both Ray's financial issues and the expansion of McDonald's. What Ray heard from Sonneborn would radically shift Ray onto a completely different career path.

Sonneborn explained to Ray that he was going about the franchising all wrong. Sonneborn explained that instead of Ray only selling franchisees the rights to McDonald's he should rather be buying up the land first and then leasing it to the franchisee. This would essentially turn a massive profit instead of the miserly 1.4% that had become the painful and humiliating reminder to Ray of all his hard work going unseen financially. Ray took up the idea and loved it. From a salesman struggling in the sales game, Ray Kroc would become a major player in the property business. And with that, he would only be just starting out on the upward trajectory that would place him amongst some of the most influential men of the era.

After all the years of struggling and waiting for the next big opportunity, Ray was, at the advice of Sonneborn, heading in the direction that he had so badly been craving. The new strategy would become something that would completely shift Ray's career aspirations. This new way of going about franchising the company would make Ray feel a lot more at ease and comfortable knowing a vast amount of money would be flowing in, allowing for the sustainability of McDonald's Corporation to continue upwards and stay that way for the foreseeable future.

This one suggestion made Ray the man as we know him today. This was Ray Kroc's one moment to tightly grab hold of the reigns of McDonald's and steer it in the direction that he wanted it to go yet never had the financial security to do so. This was another one of the opportunities that Ray Kroc would see and make the most of. And undoubtedly, that is exactly what he would go on to do. Sonneborn may have been the financial genius behind the new plan, but Ray put it in motion and got the ball rolling. He saw it as something that he would regret if he did not take this one chance. And that was something he realized he could not live with if he did not take his chances and go for it.

Things had not been easy for Ray, especially with Dick and Mac constantly shooting down his ideas. He had grown apart from the small idea of just franchising McDonald's. What Ray wanted to do was so much more than just that, and in order for him to be able to effectively carry out what he had initially set out to do, he needed them to agree. And in turn, things had started to become increasingly delicate in terms of his professional relationship with Dick and Mac.

However, there would be one more snag in the sheet before Ray could implement Harry Sonneborn's genius suggestion. This would be a decision that would not be easy for Ray to make, but it would go on to be the only logical way forward for the steady growth of McDonald's. Ray had seen this coming for a while… now he had to go through with it.

1961: The Big Year

1961 would prove to be a pivotal year for Ray and McDonald's. For Raymond Albert Kroc, the tumultuous ride in his personal life began to show up prominently. His marriage with Ethel was starting to break down even further. Ray's biggest flaw was that he couldn't stop. He chased dreams and chances and that put him at a disadvantage when it came to knowing that "now is the time to settle down." Though this mainly applied to his career, it certainly also applied to his love life. While on a business trip to meet up with a franchisee at his other restaurant, Rawland "Rollie" Smith, Ray, accompanied by Fred Turner (Operations Vice President and a former McDonald's grill operator in 1956) noticed a beautiful blonde-haired woman sitting at a piano, playing to the crowd. He was so transfixed by her that everything was slowly drifting away in his vision except for her. The woman, Joan Beverly Smith, Rawland's wife, would become the one thing he needed in his life to complete it.

These conflicting feelings would follow Ray back to Illinois, where Ethel was near breaking point. Their marriage had become frayed over the years, especially when Ray got involved with McDonald's. Ethel did not like that he was away so much and she also did not have the same vision as Ray about McDonald's and how it could revolutionize the food industry. She just did not get it; why it had become such an obsession for him and why he decided to jump into something so late in his life. She wanted to see her husband, not wonder when he'd be home. Ray understood - they had been married for thirty-nine years. But he still had feelings inside that he could not bear anymore. He described his marriage with Ethel as a wonderful time that even gave him a child, but that the door between them had closed. He just could not shake off the thought of Joan, probably because they had started having an affair. With his interests growing far and wide, Ray realized he had a cloud over his head, seeding an awful feeling of self-doubt. In 1961, the big year for Ray, he and Ethel got divorced.

It is unclear whether or not Joan was the main reason he and Ethel were divorced, but we know it's one of the main reasons Ray had changed. He had outgrown his past life and he needed people around him who matched his ambition. Joan was one such person. She had a volatile personality, same as Ray, and he loved her for it. She was strong and had a mind of her own. He appreciated a woman like that.

Meanwhile, as the intense storm of divorce raged on, Ray and Joan planned to go to Las Vegas to get married, but Joan got cold feet and retreated back to the security of her husband, Rawland. Something changed for Joan as things started to become more and more real. She truly did love Ray, but she realized what kind of man Ray was and this alone could have seeded doubt in her mind. Keep in mind that Joan was twenty years Ray's junior, and that age gap could have accounted for many a seed of doubt. Joan, like Ethel, wanted stability. Ray needed Joan to steady the rocking ship that kept him afloat. He was deeply affected by her admission of doubt and the end of their affair, but he didn't let that stop him. He still had his first love - McDonald's.

So, as his romantic life was going through multiple hardships, Ray wanted to grow McDonald's even more, much to the contempt of Dick and Mac, who by this time had started seeing Ray as a pariah, a man who had come into their lives only to ruin what they had. They had become just as frustrated with Ray about his advances for more money as Ray was about them being too stingy. For Dick, patience was key to seeing success, but Ray was always adamant that there wouldn't be another time to get this or that done or completed. It's safe to say that there was friction, tension, and charged emotions when it came to these differences of opinion. A crossroads had emerged where the differences in personality and ambition underlined the deteriorating relationship between both parties. The brothers McDonald felt as if Ray was taking over their business, which is exactly what Ray was planning to do.

During this time, in the 1960s, new fast-food chains were popping up everywhere, seemingly copying the model that McDonald's had created. Kroc, as always, spoke of McDonald's as the best and that these new startups were the rest. He said that they could not match the same quality, the same service, nor the same cheap prices that had made McDonald's such a success. He was deadpan in his belief that the new startups, such as InstaKing (Burger King today), Kentucky Fried Chicken, Arby's, and Hardee's would not be as popular or successful as McDonald's. He believed that the name alone - McDonald's - was enough. Hook, line, and sinker.

But this made Ray's level of frustration with Dick and Mac soar even higher. The brothers had only wished to maintain a small number of restaurants, not the nationwide campaign of shock and awe that Ray had insisted was in the best interests of everybody involved in the franchise. The brothers became annoyed with Ray for wanting to make changes to the original blueprint that they had set in stone. Ray became even more desperate, sending the brothers letters, but to no reply. This made Ray realize just how much they both lacked in vision. He started this thing and he wasn't going to let two ungrateful men ruin that for him.

1961 was also the year that Ray had finally had enough of Dick and Mac. The two modest brothers had become so much smaller than the vision of McDonald's which was already realizing itself. Ray just didn't understand how the brothers could not be on board with the new McDonald's. They didn't share the same values as Ray, and Ray believed that McDonald's was McDonald's because of how hard he worked to get the franchise up and running. Ray took a lot of credit for building McDonald's, which in itself is not the wrong way to look at it. He went behind their backs often, and the brothers would only hear about it once whatever he did was finished, which angered them. By this point, Dick and Mac had had enough of Ray and they wanted him gone, but it would not be easy for them, and when Ray came along with an offer to buy out McDonald's from them, they were absolutely astounded. How could this vile man sweep in and take their name? But that's what Ray wanted. He wanted all of it. The years of struggling, his divorce, his vision - they all molded into one singular goal: total control over the McDonald's name.

Harry Sonneborn helped Ray find the funds for the purchase. The price, however, was a mammoth one. Dick and Mac were devastated by this proposal to purchase, but one can look into their past where they promised each other that they would be millionaires by fifty. They decided, after putting aside the pain, that they wanted $2.7 million each. Why does that number look a bit different? Well, that's because Dick and Mac wanted a million each after taxes… and in cash. Ray was bowled over by the vast amount of money these small-town boys wanted, but Ray knew that this was the one window of opportunity that would allow him to finally have McDonald's all to himself, but there was one more snag. Ray was under the impression that the deal included the buying out of the San Bernardino McDonald's store, but the brothers gaffed at this. No, they said, this one we are keeping. So, relenting to their wishes, Ray handed over their million each.

The brothers took down their own name from their own restaurant. No longer were they allowed to use it. McDonald's belonged to someone else and now it had come to this. Dick and Mac renamed their joint "Big M". Still annoyed at Dick and Mac for all the grief that they had given him, Ray opened up a McDonald's a block away from Big M, which eventually put Big M out of business.

This side of the story shows just how ruthless Ray Kroc could be. Some will say what he did to Dick and Mac was inhumane, while others will say to you that what Ray did was for the best; he saw the potential in McDonald's and needed to do something before that all went to hell because the brothers did not share his ambitious ideas. Which is true. Ray needed to get rid of them somehow and when Harry Sonneborn suggested an outright purchase of the whole McDonald's entity, he knew he had to do it. He had far bigger goals and objectives than Dick and Mac, and McDonald's was the conduit through which Ray wanted to achieve it all. He wanted to become something, he wanted to continue growing the business that he felt the brothers were neglecting with their modesty and humility. What they lacked was not just ambition but a ruthlessness which would allow McDonald's to expand far beyond the dreams Ray had for it.

The brothers had become the bain of his existence, and he was far past the normal human levels of annoyed, frustrated, and angry. He was becoming a changed man, someone who could actually achieve monumental success. And so that is why he felt he needed to get rid of the brothers. Yes, he paid them off and this made them millionaires, but Ray saw the bigger picture. The much, much bigger picture. Sadly, though, that just did not include Dick and Mac. And if $2.7 million was the price to pay and to show for it, then that was what he needed to do, and that is what he did.

All his life Ray had wanted an opportunity to change his life, to change his story. He wanted something that would culminate with a sense of contentment, something that would prove that his ambition could be bigger than his wildest imagination. He wanted success.

Ray had done it. All his life he had been trying so hard to make it. And he had definitely made it now. He could not believe that McDonald's - all of it - was his. Not a man to display his emotion, he was proud of himself. He was proud of how far he had come, so late in his life, to finally make it. But he would do as Ray Kroc always did - never stop working. Ray had complete control. And now that there were no more obstacles and hurdles presenting themselves in the form of the McDonald brothers, Ray emerged victorious after years of haggling and arguing over the contract agreement from 1954. He was able to do what he pleased, and that was to give America McDonald's, to keep giving McDonald's to the people - the good families of the United States.

In 1961, in the basement of newly-opened McDonald's in Elk Grove Village, Illinois, Ray launched a training program that would become one of the most famous pieces of work Ray did with his McDonald's franchise. This training program was titled "Hamburger University". The subject? Hamburgerology. It was at Hamburger University that franchisees were trained on how McDonald's operated: the quality, the service, and the cleanliness. It was a complete success. In Addison, again in Illinois, Ray struck a deal to use a research development lab to devise, design, and construct new methods for cooking, serving, freezing, and storing.

Ray Kroc embodied the McDonald's authenticity. After all, he did famously say, "There is a science to making and serving a hamburger."

Chapter 3

RAY KROC: FAST FOOD KING

McDonald's Corporation: Ray Kroc a Man on a Mission

With Ray now in full control over the McDonald's Corporation and its name, Ray was beginning to create strives forward in the food industry. The McDonald's name was one that was known across the United States, and that alone was the reason behind his dedication to open nearly one thousand McDonald's restaurants across the nation. He wanted to create a much larger image for the company. Ray was Danny Daydreamer, and so he wanted to open McDonald's restaurants everywhere he could - airports, stadiums, department stores, parks. He was relentless in his pursuit of trying to establish the stores everywhere. After all, that was indeed the Kroc ideology and philosophy: do something properly and succeed or do nothing and regret it later on down the road.

Ray was always looking to find new things to help make the McDonald's menu stand out. He had a few ideas himself that he put into action which unfortunately did not have the desired effect and were not a hit. He decided from that point on that he would leave the creative ideas to the professionals.

Some successes over the following years only propelled McDonald's to even greater heights, such as with the introduction of the Big Mac, which even today is still the world's most popular hamburger.

But Ray understood what it would take to continue making McDonald's a success. He was always observing and formulating plans of action to integrate into his blueprint. A studious man who wanted to make his vision come to life, he only wanted to make McDonald's the best. One thing he was so adamant about, no matter where in the world one was, was that each and every single McDonald's product tasted exactly the same as the next place. He didn't want an inconsistent rot to set in. He didn't want the franchisees, as was the case with Dick and Mac when they first tried to franchise on their own, to customize the menus. He simply would not tolerate that, and in the early years of Ray's franchising of McDonald's, menu customization was one such factor that he had to contend with, which is why he put into play a handbook for franchisees to learn from. The penalty, if the rules and blueprint were not followed to the letter, could result in the termination of the lease of that franchisee.

Ray knew what he was doing and, furthermore, what he wanted. McDonald's was on the rise and it didn't seem as if the franchise would ever stop. As it became more and more popular so too became the demand for more and more McDonald's. People became obsessed and excited by the idea of McDonald's, and that was exactly why Ray was in this now. He had invested himself into the McDonald's brand to spread the happiness that embodies itself when an individual, young or old, opened up that hot bag which contained a hamburger and fries. He wanted everyone to have that facial expression which displayed everything great that had been touched upon the taste buds. Ray actually bought into it, and he wanted folks to buy into that as well, and he worked incredibly hard to make sure that everything about McDonald's, coast to coast, was operated in the correct manner because that was the only way to ensure that the functionality of the franchise was intact and moving in perfect harmony.

With the continuous advancement of technology, Ray knew that McDonald's had to adapt to the changing times in order to maintain stability. Everything needed to be just right. There was no such thing as a shortcut and he'd be damned if anyone working for McDonald's believed that there was such a thing as shortcuts. Cutting corners was not in Ray Kroc's vocabulary, and he expected the same from grill operator to board members. He wanted everyone to operate on the exact same wavelength, the same frequency, so as not to be stumped by differing opinions. He enjoyed hashing everything out with the staff, but he also liked finding that line of balance in which to implement alterations to tailor the needs of different places and different people within them.

He understood people. That was one of the things that had always made Ray stand out amongst his peers. Ever since he was a child, people in his neighborhood in Oak Park had said he was an intelligent, charming, friendly young boy, and he had taken those values with him into adulthood. While at the paper cup company and then while selling Multimixers, everyone always turned to Ray for advice, help, or just conversation. He was outgoing and dedicated to serving the needs of other people - which is what McDonald's as a whole values itself on being able to do. In those days, of course, family stood out and was a smart "niche market" that Ray had engineered his restaurants to cater to;he wanted families to come to McDonald's, and he worked tirelessly to make that happen. Then, when it did, he worked even harder to maintain that image and reputation of being a place for families to come and enjoy. He wanted "good American families" to be the main audience for a McDonald's in every state and, later, every country. Family was the hallmark.

In 1963 Ray met Jane Green. She was a young, blonde, complementary girl. She wanted to be involved in the inner circle of the big boy's club, and Ray found this appealing. Most of all she was convenient. Within two weeks, Ray proposed to Jane and they were married. Jane, it should be said, was nearly identical to Joan.

One thing Ray stated when he first began franchising and seeing suburban areas as the main places in which to establish McDonald's restaurants was that he did not want them to be located in downtown areas. He was concerned about having poor people coming in after closing time and he had concerns about the cleanliness standards those hypothetical downtown McDonald's would be able to maintain. He knew they wouldn't work, and he also knew promoting McDonald's in poorer areas would be difficult to do, due to a host of factors surrounding it: Crime, ill-behavior, defacing of property - definitely not marketing tools for promoting a family-friendly establishment.

Focusing now on Harry Sonneborn, Ray owed Sonneborn a hell of a lot for what he had contributed toRay purchasing McDonald's. Sonneborn was a six-foot-tall, financial genius who knew the game inside out, and who had given Ray that added factor of accomplishment. Sonneborn was the one person in Ray's inner circle that Ray could go to for anything. They had grown close over the past few years. Ray felt the same way about Fred Turner, who was a grill operator at the Des Plaines, Illinois McDonald's when Ray first met him. Ray was impressed by the young man, who he saw as ambitious, and this sat well with Ray. One can only think that Ray perhaps saw a little bit of himself in Fred. Either way, Fred got promotion after promotion until, in 1958, was given the role of second-in-command by Ray.

Ray knew he could not do it all on his own, no matter how hard he tried. The true test of a leader in any spectrum - be it politics all the way down to selling ice cream on a beachfront - is to know how to delegate responsibility to maximize full-circle productivity. Ray knew that he needed people around him to help build the McDonald's empire. He didn't take all the credit for what McDonald's would become, instead insisting he was only the head of the big machine that was operated by thousands more. He was but a part of the corporation. And he never viewed anyone more equal than someone else. Everyone was the same to him, and that showed his character. He could easily talk to heads of state and he could just as easily talk to the french fries cook with the same level of respect. That shows the leader he was; it also shows what kind of man he was. Dedicated to McDonald's and dedicated to those who worked with him and worked for him, no one was beneath Ray Kroc.

At his core, Ray was the only person who could have truly built McDonald's into what it is today. One can imagine what the world would be like if he didn't make the effort to fly out to California to see the small octagonal-shaped establishment in San Bernardino, but it is because he had that drive to please people that he ended up on the crest of a wave that would eventually make him iconic. Yes, the differences between him and the McDonald brothers created tension and eventually lead to the brothers losing the rights to their own name, but in 1954, Ray saw what they wanted to do with the restaurant. They wanted to grow it, although not as wide-scale as Ray eventually envisioned it to be, and Ray was deeply attached to them. He respected them for coming up with such an innovative idea. And in part, despite their skepticism, the brothers respected Ray. They knew he could make McDonald's big, but they did not think both Ray and McDonald's would outgrow them. That was all Ray. He built something big on a tight financial leash. He risked it all and came out defying the odds to become the type of man he always wanted to be: successful.

In 1965, four years after the outright purchase of McDonald's by Ray, the 700th McDonald's franchise was opened, whilst the year of '65 also marked the 10th anniversary of the "first" McDonald's that was opened by Ray in Des Plaines, Illinois, in 1955. Ten years of continued, sustained, consistent, and monumental success, McDonald's made history once again. This time around they became one of the first fast-food chains to go public on the stock market. Offerings opened at $22.50 and the company burst into an even brighter spotlight based on how enormously it traded. This made Ray an overnight millionaire… and it kept going. And going. He could hardly believe it. As Fred Turner said, "I don't quite think he understood what it meant. It would go like, 'Ray, you made a million today. Another million. Another million".

1965 also represented the year that Ray would establish the Kroc Foundation, which was established to do medical research on diseases such as alcoholism, diabetes (which Ray suffered from), and MS (which Ray's sister, Lorraine, suffered from). Ray's younger brother, Robert, by now a renowned doctor, was head of research, a role he would relish.

Moving back to McDonald's, Ray knew times were changing. He had to adapt the company to match the times. He was incredibly open to the suggestions and opinions of the franchisees. There are well-documented instances where he would travel wherever he needed to go in order to conduct discussions with the franchisees. There they would discuss everything, and he would often have to listen to the geographical sense of these discussions. Different places mean different preferences. Different preferences meant making changes so as to cater to people's needs. And one such alteration was the sudden realization that there was a need for something else… something that would connect with one of McDonald's most prominent target markets - children.

Ray noticed how sports teams had mascots that ran along the sidelines at games, interacting with the children. The children loved it. So what if McDonald's had a mascot? Would it work? Would it appeal to both children and their parents? Would it heighten the family-focused application of the name McDonald's? Would it represent the franchise positively?

So, an experiment was conducted. Ray got in touch with a few people about the idea that had been sitting on his mind, and the green light was given. In 1965, someone appeared for the first time who would become an absolute hit: Ronald McDonald, the company's clown mascot. Originally Ronald was named Donald but Ray changed after realizing it wouldn't work so well commercially. Ronald McDonald would become one of the most recognized figures in America; a survey conducted only served to prove this, with 90% of America's children knowing who Ronald McDonald was. Ronald was everywhere. Television commercials, magazines. He was a sensation, and the McDonald's Corporation rode the wave successfully from a commercial point of view, and adults with children approved of the character.

But for Ray, this was not enough. The man from Oak Park, Illinois, had bigger aspirations for McDonald's, and he wanted to get it done and over the line. Age was beginning to catch up with him by then, but he refused to let that stop him. His attention now turned away from the US market. He had McDonald's coast to coast across the States and with that goal now accomplished, he needed to do something else that was much, much bigger. In 1967, McDonald's ventured off into the global community. Restaurants were opened in Canada and Puerto Rico, which cast a glancing eye from Europe, who were slowly being seduced by the golden M and famous hamburgers.

In 1968, Ray and Jane got divorced. Ray realized that their marriage had run its course and there was a sense of something being out of place. After five years with Jane, Ray knew what that what he really wanted. Joan swirled around on his mind and heart every single day.

Ray got his chance in 1969 when he invited Joan, and a handful of other close friends, up to his hotel room on his birthday. He was celebrating it and after bumping into Joan. She had become more beautiful. She made him feel things he had forgotten how to. He wanted to talk to her, to see her. He needed that, so Ray pulled out all the stops to win her back In his hotel room, he had a grand piano set up. He was a romantic at heart and knew that the piano would be a symbol of what they had shared with each other all those years ago. This maneuver paid off and Ray and Joan would be married until his death in 1984.

Two years passed, and with the continued popularity of Ronald McDonald, Ray decided it was time to expand on the idea of the mascot they had created. So began the campaign of commercials describing the fantasy food world of McDonaldland. A year later, in 1972, McDonaldland introduced a sleuth of new characters into its fantasy food world. Obviously, this campaign was for children - It promoted fun and imagination, and the kids loved it. One can assume Ray took notes of how well Walt Disney was doing with his incredible films and parks. Of course, adults loved it too. Many can remember the hamburger-stealing thief named Hamburglar; Grimace, the purple-clad, four-armed creature who stole milkshakes; Mayor McCheese, the burger-headed mayor of McDonaldland; and Captain Crook, a pirate captain who would steal Filet-O-Fish sandwiches (notice the reference to Disney's Captain Hook from Peter Pan). Everybody just couldn't get enough of McDonald's.

Due to such success, in all aspects of the McDonald's pipeline, the company had become a billion-dollar corporation. Ray realized just how hard he had to work to get the company there. It took everything he had, yet he remained jubilant and optimistic and unperturbed by everything. He was a strong character. One of the most iconic and important men of the 20th Century.

He had the girl. He had the money. He had everything. But still, there was something that just did not sit right in his life. Like something was still missing.

By now Ray was starting to feel something very new to him. It had been coming for a long time, but only now, so late in his life, he was beginning to feel the wear and tear of working so hard. That feeling was to stop. That feeling inside of him represented his story and for the first time in his life, he felt settled, comfortable. Complete. In 1974, at the young age of seventy-two, Ray Kroc stepped down from his position within the company, handing over the reins to Fred Turner. Though retiring, he still had a large influence over the decision-making process on the board.

Chapter 4

THE RAY KROC LEGACY

Childhood Passion: From Hamburgers to Home Runs

Ray had one burning fire inside of him that still needed realizing. He had built by far the most successful food business in the world; he had become stinking rich after putting McDonald's on the American Stock Exchange rollercoaster; he owned a hell of a lot of property; he had married the woman of his dreams. Yet there was just one thing left for Ray to accomplish in his life that had been his biggest passion since childhood. Baseball.

After Ray retired from his role at McDonald's, in typical Ray Kroc fashion, he was hungry for more. Now that he had the time and the money, he sought out new challenges in which to invest himself. The idea formulated pretty quickly into his mind that he needed to follow his heart - to invest in something his heart had a burning passion for since the days of watching the Chicago Cubs with his father.

He found out that a Major League Baseball team in California, the San Diego Padres, were for sale. However, the team had already been sold to a Washington based grocery-chain owner by the name of Joseph Danzansky. It was in Danzansky's plans that he would move the team to Washington, which had caused quite a stir. The sale of the San Diego Padres to Danzansky was overshadowed and wrapped around by lawsuits. Ray smelt the opportunity and swooped in to purchase the team for $12 million. Ray decided to keep the team in San Diego, which endeared him to the team's fanbase.

In the same year, the Padres lost 102 games, which Ray was truly embarrassed by. He saw that changes needed to be made in order to sustain the building of a team which could pose a competitive challenge at the top end of the standings. However, it should be said, that the San Diego Padres drew in mammoth crowds. People were fascinated by the spectacle of having McDonald's's founder at the helm. It was just an overall exciting time for the team.

At heart, Ray was a fan of the team and what it represented. However, on April 9th, 1974, Ray's image of a hard-working, dedicated man soared through the roof when the Padres were about to lose another game, this time to the Houston Astros in the season opener. Ray felt even more embarrassed than the team and he felt compelled to address the situation playing out on the field. He picked up the public address microphone and announced to the 39,100 fans in attendance that, "I have never seen such stupid ballplaying in my life!" The crowd cheered. It showed them that he wasn't just some yuppie businessman trying to make a quick buck. The fact that he had to apologize on the team's behalf showed he cared about the quality of the Padres' baseball which they had paid hard-earned money to see.

The years came and went and in 1979, Ray picked up a hefty fine from Major League Baseball's baseball commissioner Bowie Kuhn for not so subtly showing an interest in Joe Morgan and Graig Nettles, two players at the end of their contracts who were about to become free agents. This fine sat in the region of $100,000. Eventually, though, Ray's frustration with the team began to show and he was tired of the unconvincing results. Ray handed over the day-to-day operations of the San Diego Padres to his son-in-law Ballard

Smith. Ray had said at the time, "There's more future in hamburgers than baseball."

Ray's mark on the Padres was instant, dating back to the day he purchased the team. After Ray died in 1984, the San Diego Padres wore a special patch commemorating his life. The initials "RAK" were emblazoned in the center of the patch. That year the San Diego Padres won the National League pennant and played in the '84 World Series. Ray, who had been so dedicated to the team over the five years of his career in baseball management, was recognized in 1999 as he was posthumously inducted into the inaugural class of the San Diego Padres' Hall of Fame.

Writing, Philanthropy, and Watching McDonald's Grow

In 1979, now free from the tiresome and frustrating work with the San Diego Padres, Ray set about working on an autobiography, which would later be titled "Grinding It Out". The project would be helped by the writer Robert Anderson. The book provided Ray with the platform to explore his own life and to then share that with the world, who knew him universally as the owner of McDonald's but not as Ray Kroc the man, the father, the husband. He would be as true to his core beliefs as possible, and his account of his life was vivid and detailed, including pieces of his life on how he went from a salesman to an incredibly successful businessman. The book would go on to be a bestseller.

The years trudged along as they always do, and Ray was living life as full as he could. In his absence from McDonald's, the corporation, still under Fred Turner, was opening restaurants left, right, and center across America and across the world. He was proud of how well Fred had carried the company so far. For Ray himself, though, he decided to put his energy into philanthropy, along with Joan, who was running most of the charitable organizations for Ray's foundation and the McDonald's Foundation. Ray also set up the Ronald McDonald House.

Over the next few years, McDonald's continuously expanded internationally until there were McDonald's in over 32 countries, including the United Kingdom, Germany, Canada, Australia, France, Japan, and Switzerland. Their reach didn't just include these countries, but also countries like Singapore, Malaysia, and the Philippines (in the Asian market); and Brazil, El Salvador, Guatemala, and Panama (making up the South American and surrounding markets). They truly were expanding to new horizons far and wide.

Ray was an old man now and he knew it. He felt it. His health was deteriorating quickly and soon he was confined to a wheelchair. Despite this, the man continued to work as hard as he could. He just didn't want to stop.

But, on the 14th of January, 1984, at the age of 81, Ray Kroc passed away. He had had heart failure. The visionary man had finally put his pens and ideas down, closed his eyes, and finally stopped working. During his eulogy of Ray, Fred Turner said, "Ray touched us. He had a rare capacity to bring out the best in us. Ray taught us. He taught us to be diligent, to apply ourselves, to raise our self-expectations, to be enthusiastic about our endeavors, to have pride and to waste not. Ray gave us an example. He gave us an example to be generous, to be thoughtful to others, to be fair-minded, to have balance, to do nothing in excess. We admire his entrepreneurship, his competitiveness, his integrity. We loved his personality, his openness and inherent honesty, and his spontaneity…"

The World That Cherished the King of Fast Food

After his death on January 14th, 1984, the world mourned the passing of a great and ambitious man. A man who worked so hard to ensure that he provided the world with joy through food. McDonald's mourned the man who built the company into a global powerhouse. He was the father figure; he was the hero and the visionary who created an empire. So, too, was the pioneer of the fast-food industry. Every little thing Ray Kroc did was calculated. He took risks, but he was an intelligent man and never did anything which could harm or tarnish the reputation that McDonald's had built in terms of its international standing. He showed himself to be a smart businessman, an entrepreneur who had goodness within him such that all he craved was to keep producing what everyone in the world craved - McDonald's. And he ensured that they did. There comes a moment, a sad pause, when one actually takes the time to stop and think about what Ray Kroc did. He sacrificed everything to go on the adventure that would eventually lead to him becoming a multi-millionaire. He deserved every penny he made and he was worth it all.

He built, in short, an empire that spread around the world. Such was McDonald's domination that it pretty much outdid the reach of colonialism and Adolf Hitler. Sure, there are negative parallels to his operations of success, but Kroc achieved something no one else had or even could. His legacy is McDonald's.

After his passing, McDonald's didn't stop its expansion. He would have wanted it to be just the way it was - ever-changing, ever-growing. Evergreen. And that's how it played out. McDonald's continued to pioneer and dominate, with sales and profits skyrocketing continuously. It was insane -

insanely phenomenal just how much the corporation took the world by storm. Even Hamburger University graduates continued to increase. McDonald's hamburgers were voted one of the "100 Products That America Makes Best".

Ray did not create McDonald's as we know it today, but he systematically built it into the empire that continues to flourish after he took over from Dick and Mac McDonald. The legacy of Ray Kroc continues today, despite the uproar of how fattening and unhealthy the food actually is, but that's what makes it so great - not unhealthy eating - but how much joy it still brings millions around the world daily. Because of McDonald's, the food industry took notes and changed with it.

Kroc was voted one of the top 100 most important Americans of the 20th Century by Life Magazine, and that shows us again just crucial he was to the advancement of the food industry in those days which have left a mark on the industry even today in the 21st Century. He was incredible in the sense that he knew how to sell an idea. Even he would have laughed back in 1954 if someone told him just how successful both he and McDonald's would be because of his vision and persistence when he would retire in 1974.

"Behind the Golden Arches" author John Love said, "With more than 500,000 people on its payroll at any one time, McDonald's is easily one of the largest employers in the United States. Its impact on the U.S. workforce greatly exceeds its current employment, because it trains so many high school students for their first jobs." And that just proves the point: Ray Kroc knew how to get things done. Of course, it took him half his life to finally find the one big opportunity, but it is because of him that the small San Bernardino McDonald's started his brilliant vision of giving America McDonald's restaurants from coast to coast. I don't even think he thought at the time that

McDonald's would be so successful that it would not just be solely focused on and in America, but the world over as well.

Ray was a visionary, and the little four-year-old boy staring up at the phrenologist who told him he would be in the food industry couldn't have imagined that, instead of just being in the food business, he would go on to revolutionize it and become the king of the industry. The thing about Ray was that, even when he was a salesman, he provided and catered to people's needs. He contributed to making his customers' lives better and easier and this value continued and followed him when he began franchising McDonald's. Ray wanted to give back. He was an open-minded and kind man, and the world today lacks because of his absence.

CONCLUSION

Ray Kroc achieved the success that he worked so hard to get. Throughout his life, he had been waiting, waiting for that one opportunity that would radically change his life. In 1954, in San Bernardino, California, he found that opportunity. McDonald's was just a single octagonal-shaped establishment on the corner of a street. Ray would turn it into a franchise, one that would span the whole of the United States of America and then the world.

From his childhood, he displayed the qualities of someone who could make it in the world. He became a salesman and worked extremely hard to provide for Ethel and for his daughter. He worked hard so he could be something. When he saw that little McDonald's, packed with people - no, families - that spoke to Ray on such an emotional level. After hearing the McDonald brothers' story, he instantly became so connected to the McDonald's idea that he literally risked everything in his life, from his house and his money to his marriage, in order to take hold of the opportunity that was presented to him and to make it work. He invested his livelihood into something that he saw as unique, and that he saw as special. He wanted to give that to children and adults around the country because he saw what the McDonald's brand stood for.

When he eventually bought out McDonald's from Richard and Maurice McDonald for $2.7 million in 1961, Ray didn't do as he pleased with the franchise. He only ratified and drilled home those values which it stood for following its renovation. Ray had not only bought McDonald's, but he bought into the idea of McDonald's. He bought into the philosophy, the mission statement: Quality, Service, Cleanliness. He revolutionized the fast-food playing field. He bested the competitors tenfold, and then still continued to build the brand and the franchise until the name was so universally recognized that it finally made Ray realize what he had actually accomplished. Yet even in his seventies, Ray Kroc did not for one single second sit back and enjoy the spoils which he had earned. He just kept on working. Even after he retired from McDonald's, the Major League Baseball team, San Diego Padres, which he purchased in 1974, offered him further challenges in which to test himself in. He didn't get the desired results that he craved from that new adventure, but he loved every second of it and left with his head held high.

What Ray certainly never lacked was the drive that most hard-working Americans possess. He never allowed anything to get in the way of achieving his dreams, and that is a prime example of a good role model for any aspiring entrepreneur. He defied the odds time after time after time, and he continued to do so. What is most amazing about him was that he only really started getting everything going when he was fast approaching his sixties. He proved that age is just a number and that age cannot affect the dreams that you have. Ray made sure he never let anyone down, and for him, that was what he prided in people. He wanted people to match his ambitious nature; he wanted people to be on his level . Bear in mind that Ray Kroc did not even finish high school yet he still defied all odds to become a successful and wealthy businessman. He never fretted over the small things and he didn't allow anything to stop him.

A part of him must have felt a bit disconnected from the world while he was trying to build a platform with which to share so much joy with that very world. He must have felt at times as if he was trapped in a bubble, his deep affection for building McDonald's becoming his sole focus and obsession leaving him drained. We know he did not externalize this emotion because that simply was not who he was. He was a strong man and kept going. He kept going and kept going. Did he struggle? Sure. He suffered from arthritis and diabetes, yet he still carried out his project with great dedication and no self-doubt of his ability. He was the 20th Century business equivalent of Hercules because the man's efforts were Herculean. He struggled through his own pain and afflictions to create something in the world for people to enjoy.

Was he innovative? Of course. Although the model of McDonald's was not his idea, he did make adjustments and renovations by designing the idea to franchise and then expand internationally. When one thinks of the small San Bernardino restaurant, sitting like a beautiful gem on the shores of some exotic beach, it is hard to imagine anyone taking just that one restaurant and growing it into one of the world's largest fast-food chains. It speaks volumes of the innovation, the genius, that Ray Kroc possessed to be able to even mentally visualize such a thing. But he did and he cultivated an absolute wonder to behold.

He had some bad traits, such as the affair he had with Joan, but he was human and was infatuated. Love does crazy things to people, and Ray was not exempt from this notion. But he didn't let the heartbreak of her leaving him stand in his way and, because of that, he became a millionaire. He built McDonald's even further above ground until it was just about touching fast food heaven. He continued to believe in his project and he did extremely well to get it just where he wanted it to be.

When he passed away in 1984, it was a sad day. But one can only imagine that Ray Kroc left the earth with a little wink, a charming smile, telling everyone why McDonald's is indeed the best place to go with your family, friends, and everyone.

Printed in Great Britain
by Amazon

RAY KROC BIOGRAPHY

The *"Founding Father" of McDonald's*

Thomas Stewart